AF439552

POWER, MOMENTUM AND COLLISIONS

**Physics for Kids
5th Grade
Children's Physics Books**

Speedy Publishing LLC

40 E. Main St. #1156

Newark, DE 19711

www.speedypublishing.com

Copyright 2017

I n this book, you will be learning about Power, Momentum and Collisions and how they relate to physics.

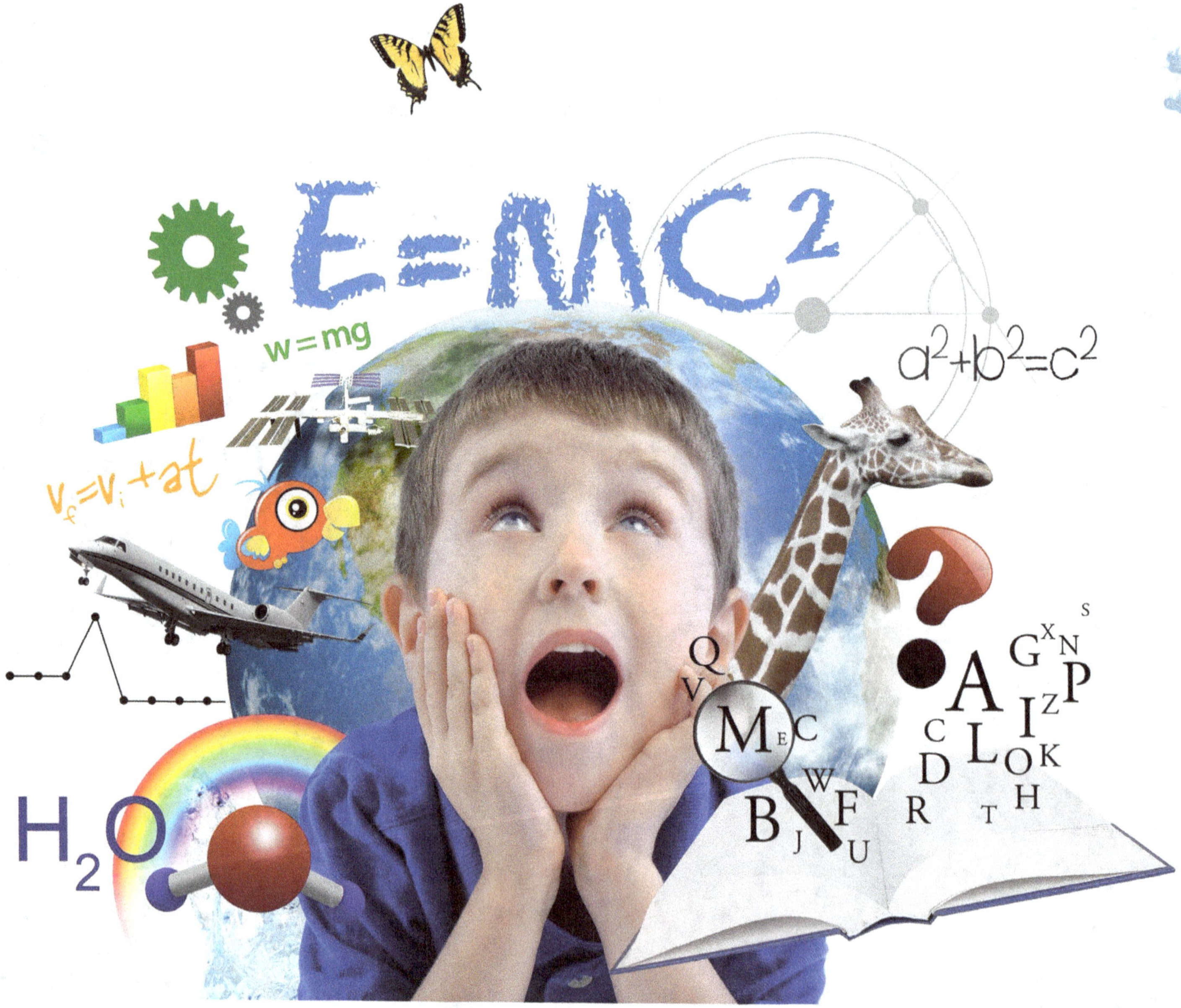
E=MC2
w=mg
a2+b2=c2
vf=vi+at
H2O
Q V M E C W B J F U A G X N S P Z I C L D O K R T H

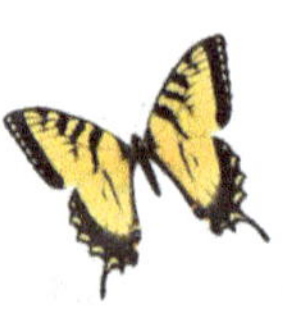

Physics is the science of studying matter and its motion and how it relates to energy and forces. There are several branches of physics that includes light, sound, waves, motion, astronomy and electricity. Physics is the study of the tiniest elementary atoms and particles and the biggest stars and the universe.

Physicists are scientists whose expertise is in the world of physics. They use a scientific method for testing hypotheses and then develop the scientific law. Albert Einstein and Isaac Newton are only two of the many famous scientists who were considered in history to be physicists.

SCIENCE
TO DAY

WHY IS PHYSICS SO IMPORTANT?

The explanation of how our world works is known as physics. Most of the technologies of today relate to scientific discoveries that were made using physics. Physics assist engineers in designing electronics, buildings, cars and airplanes.

PHYSICISTS CHECKING THE ELECTRONIC COMPONENTS

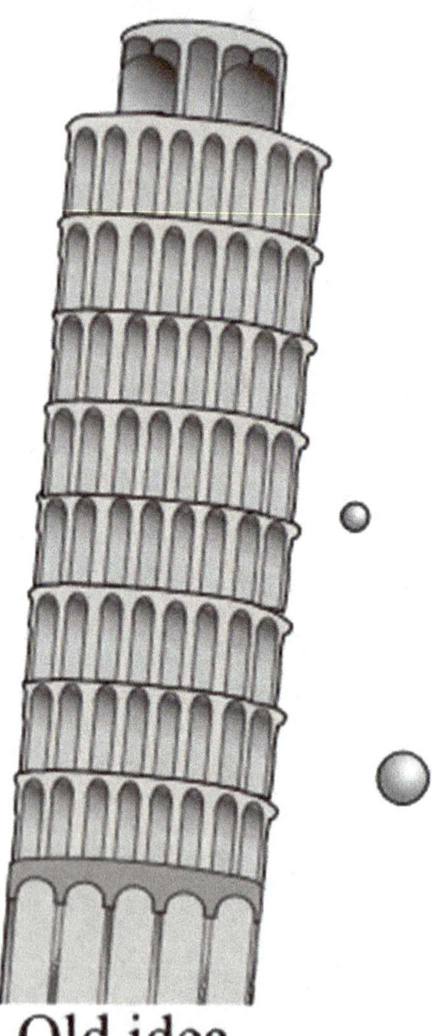

THE LEANING TOWER OF PISA EXPERIMENT

SOME OF THE IMPORTANT PHYSICS DISCOVERIES

- The discovery that the Earth rotated around the sun was made by Nicholas Copernicus.

- The Leaning Tower of Pisa experiment, as demonstrated by Galileo, found that objects heavier than light ones would not fall faster.

- The discovery of how gravity works and the three laws of motion were published by Isaac Newton.

- The description of the atom and the atomic theory of matter was completed by John Dalton.

- The theory of relativity was published by Albert Einstein.

- The quantum theory was written by Max Planck.

HOW GRAVITY WORKS BY ISAAC NEWTON

A KID KICKING THE BALL WITH POWER

POWER

Sometimes you might see the word "power" used in describing someone with authority, such as a dictator or king. It is also used for describing something or someone that is strong, such as a football player that gets a touchdown. With physics, it is used for describing the rate at which the energy is used. It can be considered a way to measure how quickly you are consuming the energy.

The equation for describing power is known as: Power = Work ÷ Time or P = W/t

Example:

- Whether you walk up a flight of stairs in 40 seconds, or can run up the same flight of stairs in 5 seconds, you are

still doing the equal volume of work. Nevertheless, you are performing it at another rate. When you are running up the stairs you are working faster. Thus, as you run up the stairs, you are working at a higher power than when walking up the same stairs.

f the amount of work involved in climbing these stairs is 1000 joules, then we calculate that power in these two scenarios P1 (running) and P2 (walking):

Power = W/t
P1 = 1000 J ÷ 5 s
P1 = 200 W
P2 = 1000 J ÷ 40 s
P2 = 25 W

As you can tell, while running, the power was quite a bit higher than while walking up the stairs.

MEASURING POWER

The Watt is the unit that is standard for measuring power. As seen in the equation shown on the board, power is the result from the equation Work ÷ Time. Joule (J) is the unit for work, so Watt is identical to J/s or joule/second.

Power = W/t

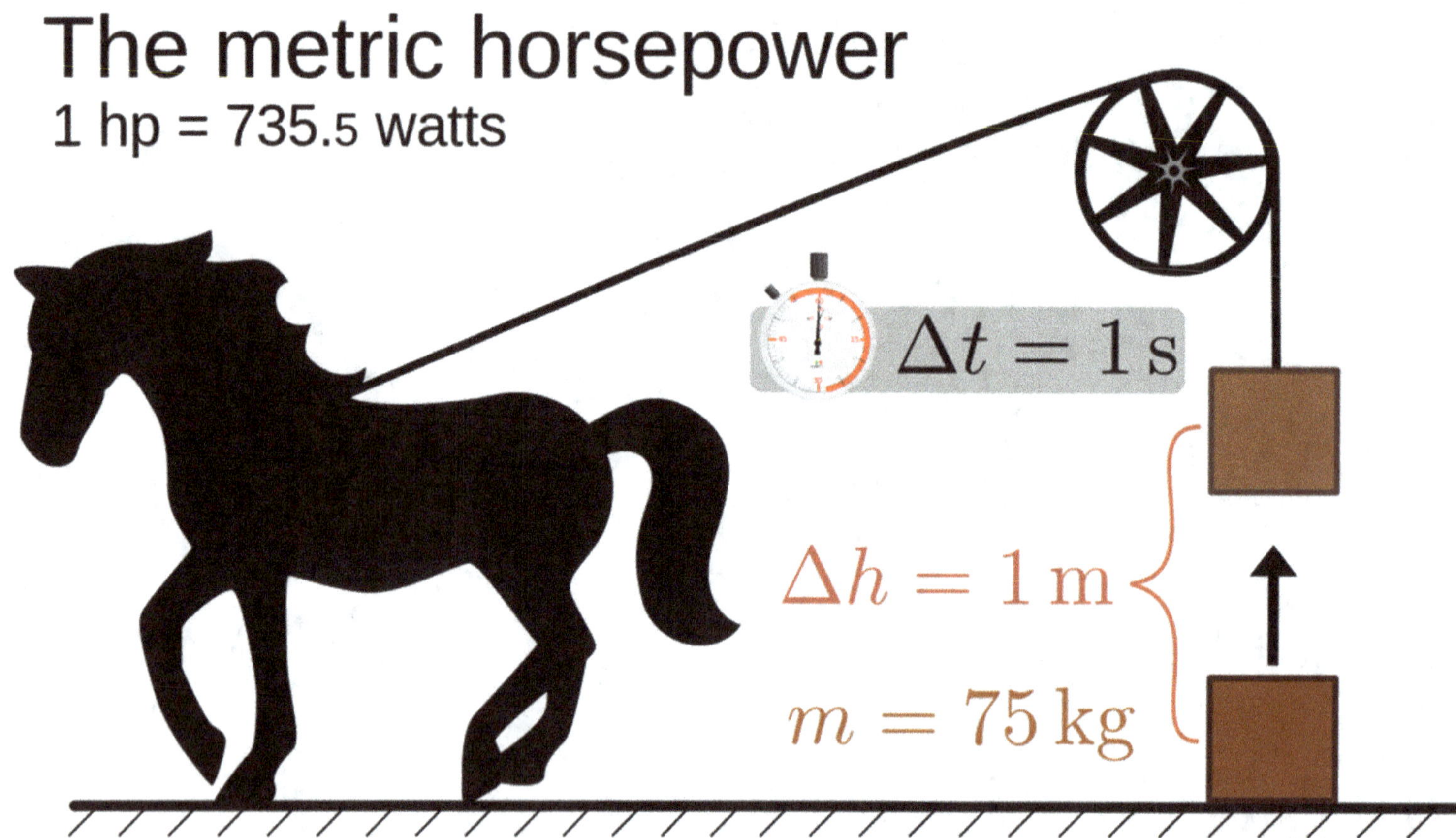

The metric horsepower
1 hp = 735.5 watts
$\Delta t = 1\,\mathrm{s}$
$\Delta h = 1\,\mathrm{m}$
$m = 75\,\mathrm{kg}$

Another unit that is commonly used for power is horsepower, which is used for machines and automobile engines. One horsepower is equal to approximately 745.7 Watts. One horsepower equals the power necessary to lift 550 pounds one foot up in one second.

HOW TO CALCULATE POWER

Power is calculated using the velocity and force of an object with this equation:

power = force x velocity

m·a_n = α
y
A;B
y = cos x
= Σ p(w)
x

ELECTRICAL POWER LINES

HOW TO CALCULATE ELECTRICAL POWER

Use the voltage and the current in attempting to figure out electrical power. Voltage is measured by volts (V) and current is measured by amperes (A). Current is noted in equations using an "I".

Power = Current * Voltage P = I * V

Example:

What is the resulting power from an electrical circuit that generates 4 amperes at 10 volts?

$P = I * V$
$P = 4A * 10V$
$P = 40$ Watts

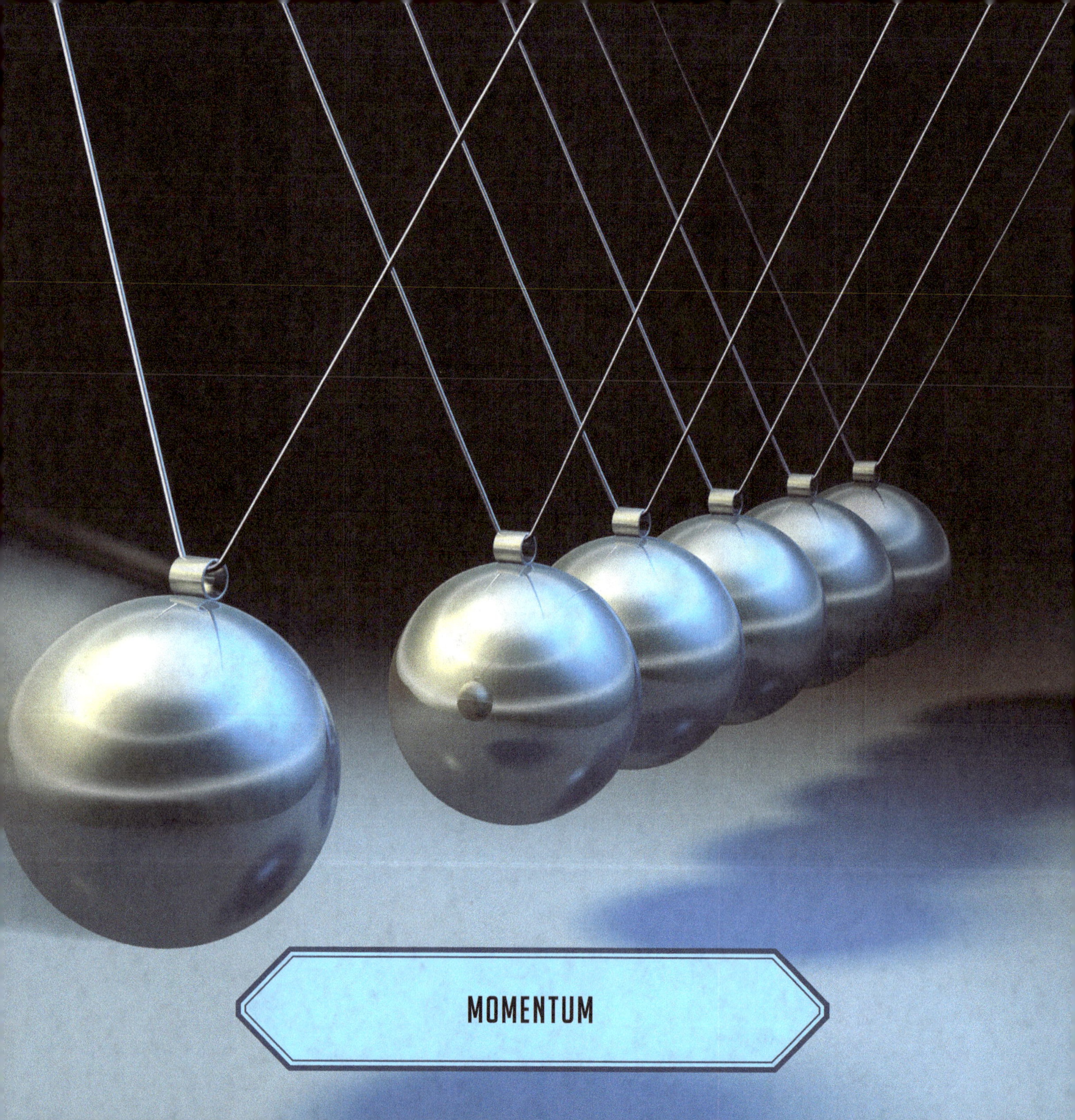
MOMENTUM

MOMENTUM

Momentum is how we measure mass that is in motion. Any moving object will have momentum. Under the law of physics, the object's momentum equals mass times velocity.

momentum = mass * velocity

Typically, momentum is abbreviated with the letter "p" as seen in the equation below:

$$p = m * v$$

The letter p is momentum, m is mass, and v is velocity.

As you can tell using this equation, both the object's velocity and its mass will have the same impact on the total momentum.

FIAT
EH·380JY
GuessGuess

You will have more momentum when running than when walking. Also, if a bicycle and a car travel down the street at equal velocity, the car will have the most momentum.

You may wonder why "p" is the letter used for momentum. No one knows for sure, but it may have come from "petere" which is the Latin word for "go towards". The letter "m" was already being used for mass, so they could not use it.

An impulse is a change in momentum.

MEASURING MOMENTUM

Typically, momentum is measured using newton-second (Ns) or kilograms times meters per second (kg*m/s).

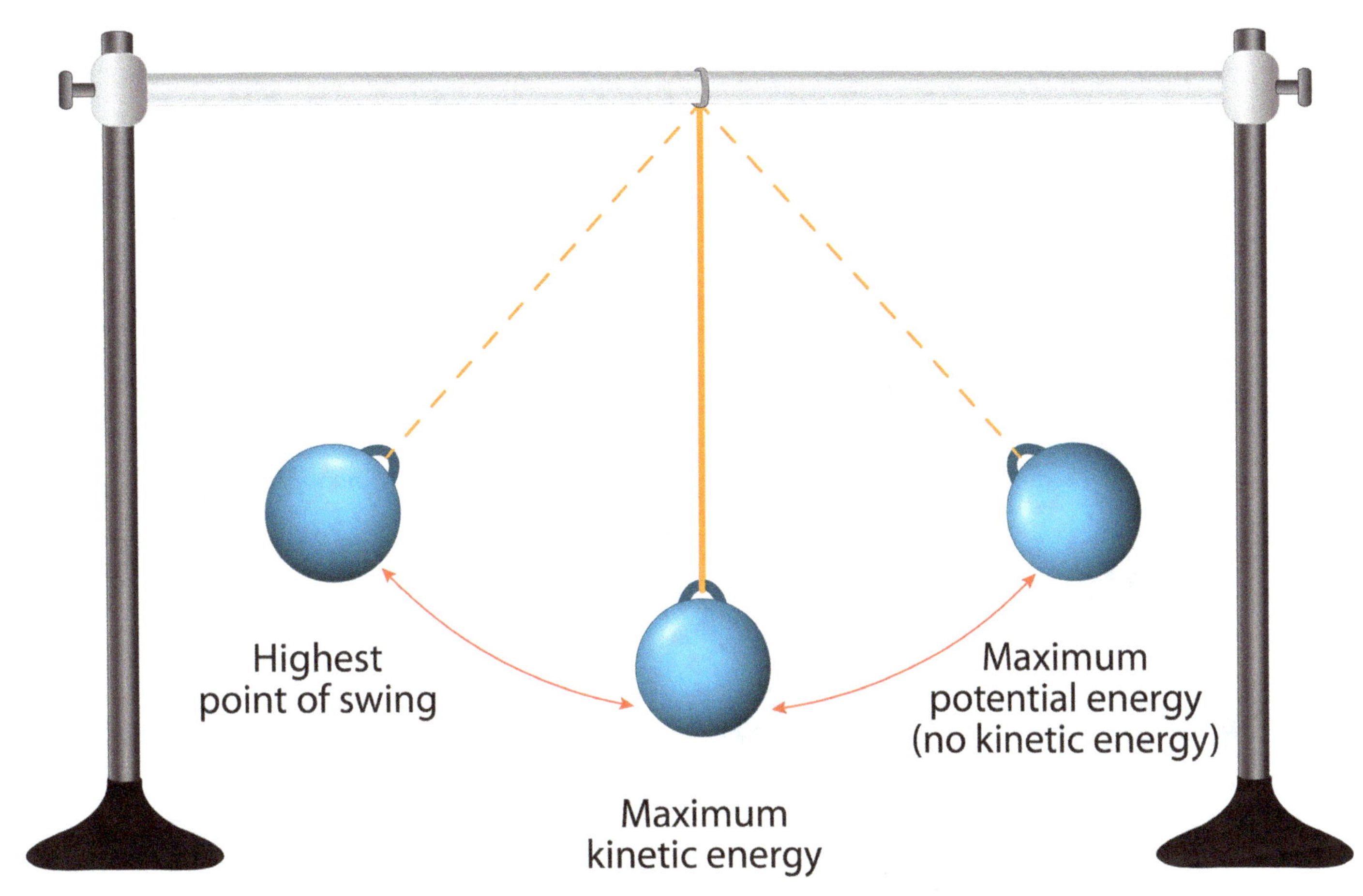

CONSERVATION OF ENERGY

IS MOMENTUM A VECTOR?

Since velocity is considered to be a vector, momentum is considered a vector as well. What this means is that momentum has the significance of momentum (which is given by $p = m * v$), and also has a direction. The momentum direction indicated by a vector or an arrow.

A collision occurs when two objects hit one another. Under the laws of physics, a collision does not need to involve an accident (similar to two cars hitting one another), but can be any type of event involving two or more moving objects exerting forces on one another for a short time period.

BOWLING

COLLISION BETWEEN POOL BALLS

Examples of a collision:

- Fingers tapping the keys of a keyboard
- One ball hitting another one on the pool table
- Baseball bat striking the ball

An elastic collision occurs when two objects have the same total kinetic energy after the encounter as they did prior to the encounter. Collisions between atoms are elastic collisions.

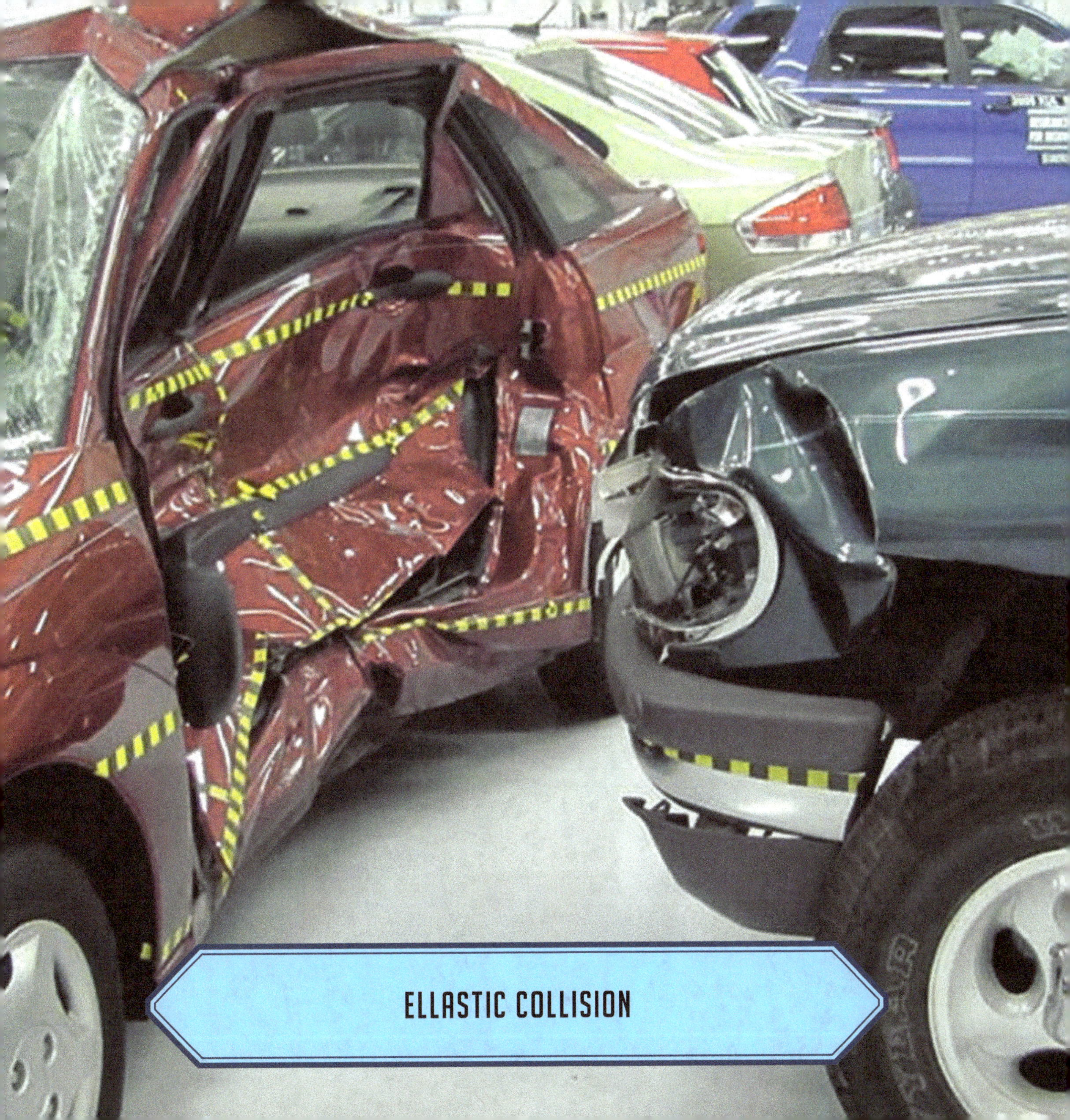

ELLASTIC COLLISION

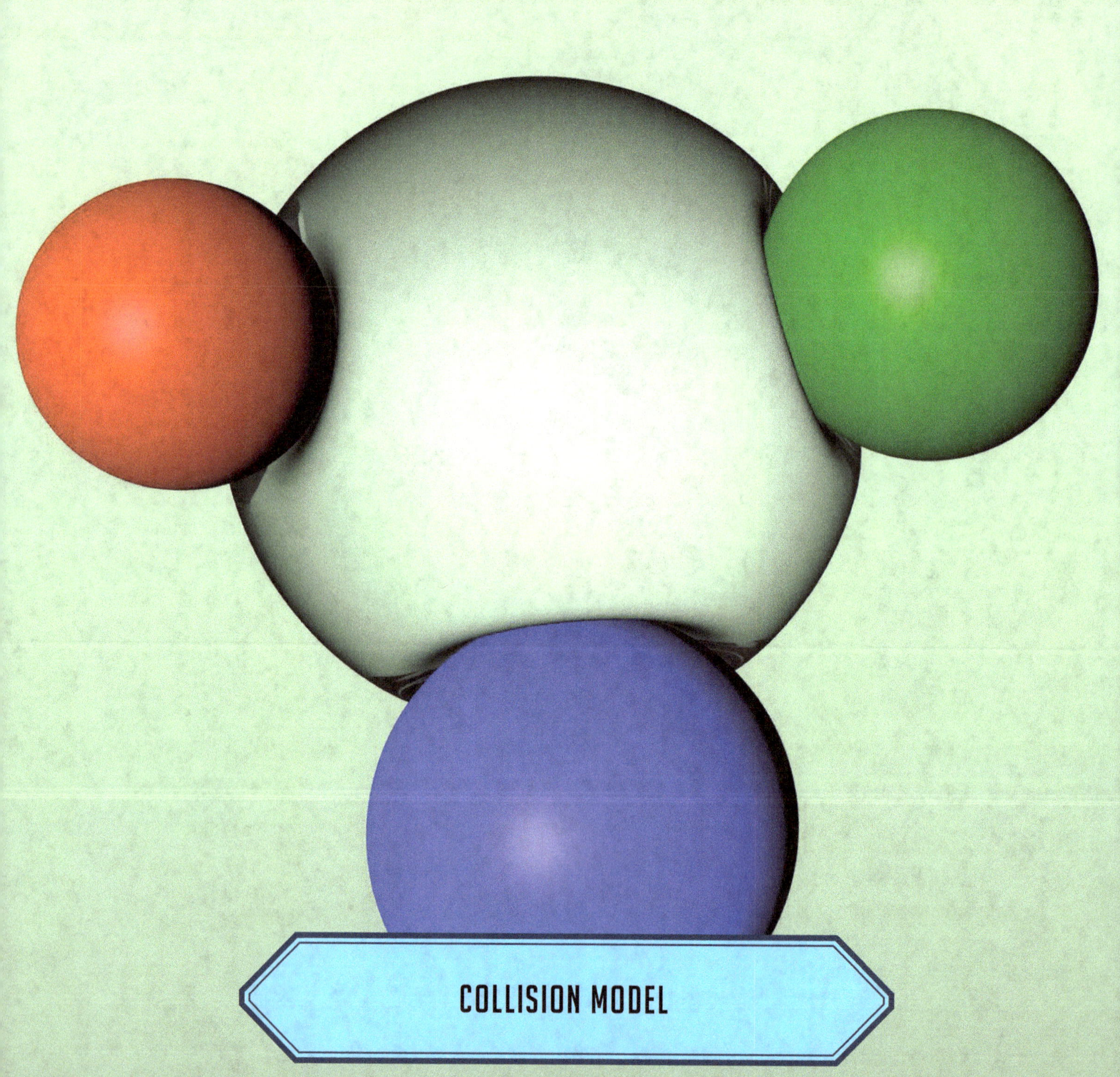

COLLISION MODEL

WHAT IS AN INELASTIC COLLISION?

An inelastic collision occurs when the kinetic energy of a collision is not conserved because of the internal friction. The molecules of a liquid or gas generally do not experience a perfect elastic collision since the kinetic energy is transferred between the molecules.

THE CONSERVATION OF MOMENTUM THEORY

This is a significant theory in physics. It defines what will happen to the momentum as two objects collide with each other.

This law asserts that as two objects collide in a system that is isolated, the total momentum of these two objects prior to the collision equals the total of them after the collision occurs. While each object's momentum may be altered, the total has to remain identical.

CAR COLLISION

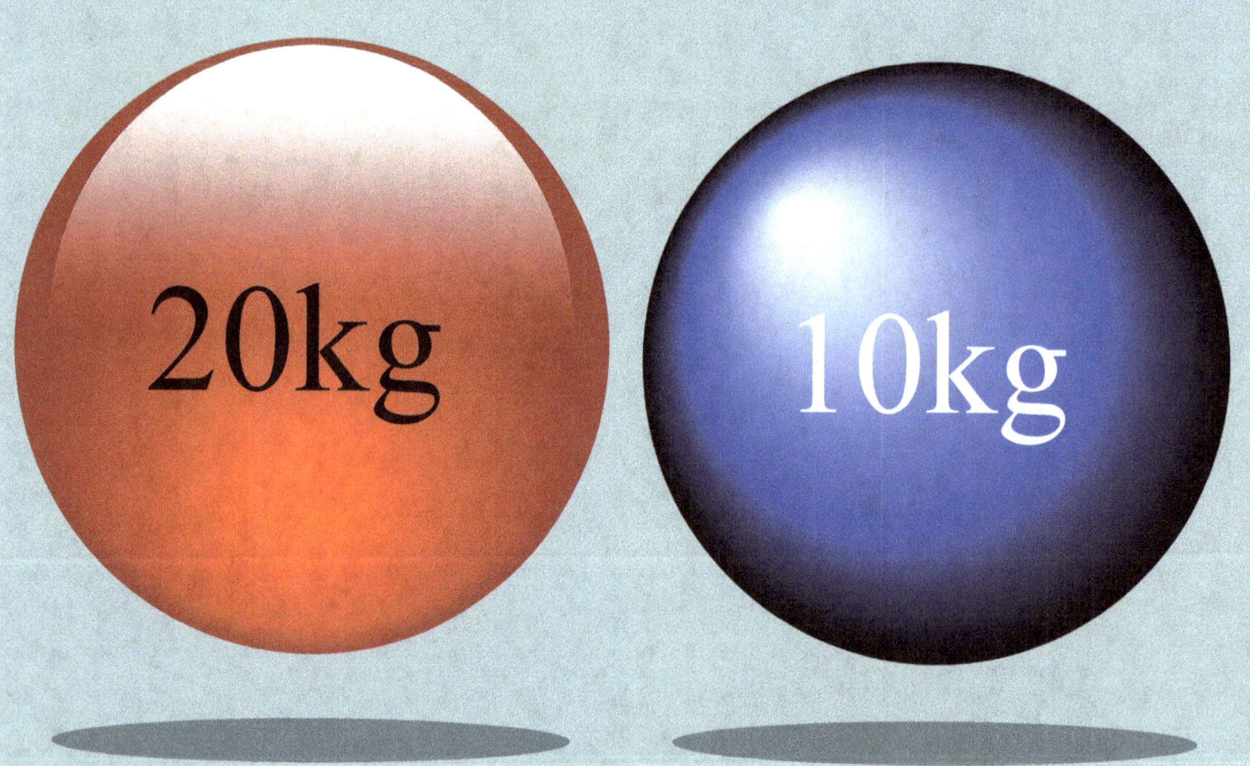

20kg
10kg

Example:

If a blue ball containing a mass of 10 kg travels east at the speed of 5 m/s and has a collision with a red ball containing a mass of 20 kg that travels west at the speed of 10 m/s, what is the resulting momentum?

We first need to find out each ball's momentum prior to the collision:

- Blue ball = 10 kg * 5 m/s = 50 kg m/s east

- Red ball = 20 kg * 10 m/s = 200 kg m/s west

The subsequent momentum will be:

- Both balls = 150 kg m/s west

SHOOTING A GUN

Note: If the object is standing still, its momentum is 0 kg m/s.

An example of how the conservation of momentum works would be the recoil from shooting a gun. Because of its larger mass, the gun shifts backwards at a lower velocity than the bullet you just fired.

WHAT IS VELOCITY?

An object's velocity is its position's change rate in respect to the frame of reference and is considered a time function. It is equal to the specifics of its speed and its direction of motion; i.e. 70 km/h to the north. It is considered a vital concept for kinematics, which is the division of classical mechanics describing the motion of bodies.

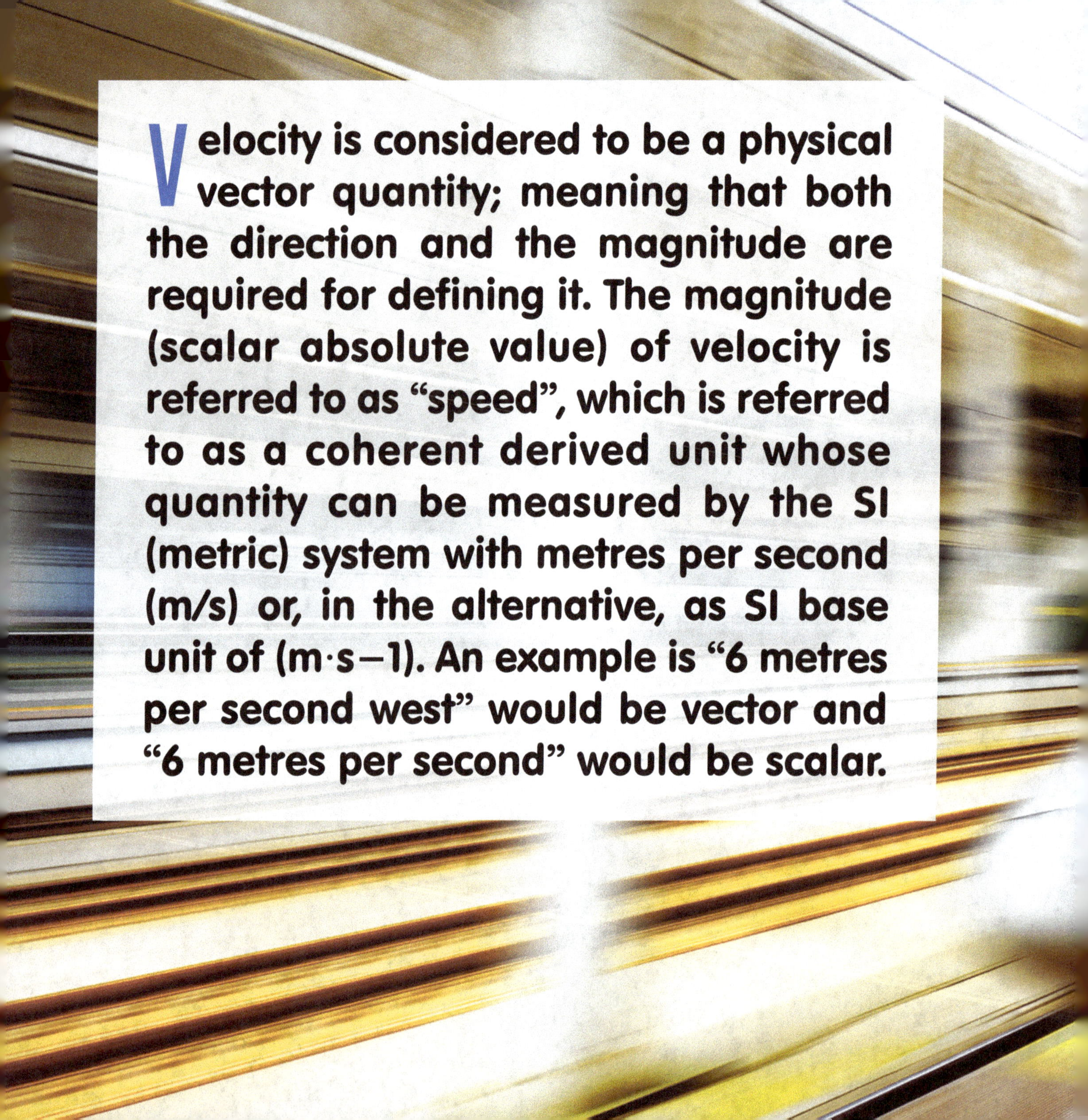

Velocity is considered to be a physical vector quantity; meaning that both the direction and the magnitude are required for defining it. The magnitude (scalar absolute value) of velocity is referred to as "speed", which is referred to as a coherent derived unit whose quantity can be measured by the SI (metric) system with metres per second (m/s) or, in the alternative, as SI base unit of (m·s−1). An example is "6 metres per second west" would be vector and "6 metres per second" would be scalar.

If a change in the object's speed occurs, either in one direction or both, it then has a velocity change and is experiencing an acceleration.

Now that you have learned the basics about Power, Momentum and Collisions, additional information can be found at your local library, by researching the internet, and by asking questions of your teachers, family and friends.

Visit
BABY PROFESSOR
EDUCATION KIDS
www.BabyProfessorBooks.com
to download Free Baby Professor eBooks and view
our catalog of new and exciting Children's Books